Lye Waste

A Very Horrible History

T Jones

DEDICATION

Thank you to Mum, Dad and Alan for all their help
with editing and photographs for this book.
And giving me the idea in the first place.

Lye Waste – A Very Horrible History

Foreword

We have all heard of Sawney Bean, the notorious Scottish murderer who was thought to murder and cannibalise travellers. How much of this is truth and how much is folklore or a propaganda plot to denigrate the Scottish, we shall never know. But a less well known tale is the horrible history of Lye Waste. If you have lived in or around Lye for a while, you probably think you know the area well. I thought I did. That is, until I attended a few talks by the Lye Historical Society and started to hear a bit about Lye Waste, only a bit, mind, as no one really seemed to want to talk about it. This aroused my interest and started me looking at the horrible history of Lye Waste. Is this a conspiracy by the people of Lye to hide their less than pleasant history? As a Wooldridge by birth, I know this unpleasant history no doubt is my history too.

Before I start, I should point out there is no cannibalism (that we know of) in this tale.

Where is Lye Waste?

Lye lies where two main roads cross, the Dudley to Pedmore Road and the Halesowen to Stourbridge Road. This crossroads is still known as Lye Cross. Lye was originally called Lyegh, Lee or Leech around 630. A Ley or Lay in Saxon times referred to a clearing or pasture, so Lye was a modified version of this. Ley is a term used in many local names, such as Dudley, Hagley and Cradley. Lye has also been refered to as Ye Lye and Lye Hamlet.

Before the early 17th century, Lye was a rural settlement. There were some big houses and farms, but most were smaller homes and cottages, where servants and farm labourers lived. In 1625, maps show Lye and in 1650, there were only a few scattered houses. But by 1699, there were 103 houses in Lye Waste (Neale, 2011)

To the east of Lye Cross was a large area of common land. It was considered waste land because of the large clay deposits, which made it unsuitable for grazing. It became known as Lye Waste. But it is perhaps best known as "Mud City."

"The area east of the Parish Church was uncultivated until the 1600s, and known as Lye Waste and Waste Bank. It gradually became a sort of shanty town of mud built houses, often called "Mud City"." (Lane, 2004)

The Original Settlers of Lye Waste

A poem quoted in Perrins describes the people of Lye Waste and the area –

"Lye, Lye Waste & Careless Green,

the three worst places ever seen

A red brick church and a wooden steeple,

a drunken parson and wicked people"

(Quoted in Perrins)

But who were they and where did they come from? The early 17th Century was a time of great upheaval due to the English Civil War. Around the 1650s, poor settlers and gypsies came to settle in an area about half a mile from the centre of Lye. They were described as *"rough and uncouth"* (Linell, 2008).

The civil war led to an increased demand for iron. The new settlers began to use clay and coal from the Lye area to produce iron goods. Because of this, they were allowed to stay (Wootton, 2008, Weston and Price, 2010)

By 1813, there were 254 families living in Lye, with 287 living in Lye Waste. By 1861, there were 5255 people, increasing to 7000 in 1866. Over 70% of the population were over 18. And there were 53 pubs. You do the maths on how many people to a pub.

It is all very well looking at the facts and figures, but what about the people of Lye Waste themselves?

They have been described as a

"population of a very peculiar description" (Anonymous)

and showing a

"marked distinction in manners and the general state of society" (Anonymous).

"....the Lye Wasters failed to integrate with their Lye neighbours, by whom they were regarded as a lawless and Godless lot."

(Dunn and Wooldridge, 2013)

They were a close knit community, but what was so wrong with the people of Lye Waste? Rumours abound about this tight knit community, including that they intermarried. Large families were rife in the area, but at the time larger families were more the norm than today. (Cochrane, 2013)

They were a bit *different* in other words.

It was said that this tight community did not tolerate strangers well.

"The males are naked, the females accomplished breeders. The children, at the age of three months take a singular hue from the sun and the soil which continues for life. The rags which cover them leave no room for the observer to guess the sex. Only one person upon the premises presumes to carry a belly - and he is the landlord. We might as well look for the moon in a coal-pit as for stays or white linen in The City of Mud. The principal tool in business is the hammer and the beasts of burden, the ass"... (Hutton 1806)

In a poem called The Beauties of Lye Waste, George Wooldridge gives us a clear indication as to why he didn't stay around Lye Waste too long. He

"claimed he saw Hell in Lye, so he hot-footed it back to London, he had no intention of meeting the Devil as well."

(Neale, 2011)

The Beauties of Lye Waste

George Wooldridge

(quoted in Perrins)

From London a few weeks ago I came down,
To pay a short visit to a country town,
When I came through a village which much took my taste,
And they told me the name of it was The Lye Waste.

When I entered the village, amazed I stood,
To see all the houses and shops built of mud,
And as I walked forward I could but admire
The young damsels, half naked, were hammering fire.

Men, women and children were making of nails,
They were cheerfully singing and telling droll tales,
Jolly Bacchus their god, and him only they fear,
For whenever they pray, tis for ale or strong beer.

These people are happy, they covet no riches,

There are some without shirts, and some without breeches,

In summer they build like the martins with dirt

And they've a house of their own, tho' perhaps ne'er a shirt.

Their shoes they are made out of such durable stuff,

They never wear out, its leather called buff,

Stockings of the same, they wear by their own choice,

To imitate Adam when in Paradise.

As for matrimony, these people detest,

To take each other's word, they think cheapest and best,

By no parson or priest do they stand to be tied,

But as nature directs, lie by each other's side.

I walked till a publick house came in view,

When I called and got some good ale it is true,

I sat myself down, 'twas the sign of the Swan,

And I vow that the landlord's a pleasant old man.

When gazing about me I saw a great spire,

And what church it was I began to enquire,

To whom it belonged to, or what sect of people

When I saw a great blaze burst out of the steeple.

This rather alarmed me, I stood in amaze,

Crying landlord, your church is all in a blaze,

We have no church at all, the landlord sad,

It's a shop where anvils and hammers are made.

This being curious, I walked up the village to see

What kind of a place the factory could be,

When I entered the door, I saw nine or ten fellows,

Some poking the fires and some blowing great bellows.

Next they drew from a furnace beneath the tall spire,

A salamander red hot, spitting venom like fire,

The men all prepared when they spied him coming,

And with great iron battles they gave him a drumming.

Though he seemed to resent it with venom so fast,
Which he poured out upon them, they killed him at last,
To see him quite conquered it pleased me right well,
But the next place I came to, they told me was hell.

I looked round in affright, and espied a deep pit,
And three or four devils at the bottom did sit,
Their faces were black, and when me they did see,
Said if I would come down they no harm would do me.

Curse your kindness though I, but nothing did say,
So I took to my heels and scampered away,
With great luck I escaped, and by heaven I swore,
They should never catch me near hell any more.

So you could say the people of Lye Waste were a bit unusual. Their irregular lifestyle led to local respectable people to call them peculiar, savages and even inbred (Pritchard) or even *"a dirty, squalid, immoral, lecherous, drunken, thieving bunch of heathens"*, who were *"mostly dirt poor Nailers"* (Neale, 2011).

The local people did not seem to have a lot of good to say about the inhabitants of Lye Waste.

Around the 1660s, we see names such as Adenbrooke, Beard, Challenor, Cox, Butler, Hill, Hancox, Male, Reade, Round, Levall, Witton, Perrins, Sheldon, Parke, Warrenton, Wilcox, Knowles and Wurler. But these are only the people rich enough to pay taxes (Neale, 2011).

Even though they were not well regarded, the people of Lye Waste were obviously hard working. The Lye Waste area was a centre of trade and industry.

"In the first quarter of the nineteenth century the Lye was known as a wild and barbaric place......(but).....A century or so later the Waste was the largest and most important part of the Lye, the centre of trade and the name often given to the area as a whole." (Pritchard)

But these poor, hard working people lived in absolute poverty, hard to imagine today.

We hear talk from people today who remember using newspaper as toilet roll or having an outdoor privy, but the people of Lye Waste at this time suffered far worse poverty than this.

This was a hard life, but a historian at the time, Hutton (1806), stated

> "*The weak died quickly and the strong survived to grow stronger and hardier with each succeeding generation. It was a kind of "line-breeding," normally associated with the canine world - a refining process in human flesh and blood - a cruel melting-pot from which only the strongest emerged*".

So even though they were considered godless and immoral, they were obviously hard working people living in difficult conditions.

Mud City – The Housing of Lye Waste

Lye Waste was also known as Mud City. In around 1650 a group of people settled on Lye Waste. Cochrane (2013) describes them as

> *"a tribe of people of diminutive size, and innocent of the usage of civilised life, who spent their time making nails."*

These settlers built their homes out of mud. Clay was readily available in the Waste and the homes they built became known as the Lye Mud Houses. The women and children were often responsible for softening the clay. They would add water and tread the clay with their feet. Straw was then added and the clay was placed into position. When it dried, more clay was added. Their homes were virtual hovels with no sanitation or fresh water. The floor was often bare earth and the roof was sometimes thatched or turfed. They were situated around The Dock, Waste Bank and Lye Waste, leading to the area becoming known as Mud City. The people of Lye Waste often were in large families and many lived in squalor, surviving on Parish funds.

Lye Waste is

"a picture of Birmingham at the time the Britons (ie the Celts) ... alias Mud City. The houses stand in every direction, composed on one large and ill-formed brick scooped into a tenement burnt by the sun and often destroyed by the frost."

(Hudson, 1780 quoted in Dunn, 1999)

The mud houses had a *"mean appearance of their clay-built cottages.…..several caricaturing representations of the mud city"* and compared the buildings to the *"miserable cabins of the wild Irish."* (Anonymous)

"Rev Robertson was the perpetual curate of the chapel of ease at Lye from 1866 to 1875. He wrote a description of Lye Waste as he first found it: "It was in those days a poor looking place — a place that many would call squalid. The mud huts were much in evidence then. The people building them themselves, throwing up balls of mud to the father as he built or repaired the walls. The floors were of clay and the roofs thatched and the crowding was extraordinary. You did not see much of this along the main road but the back streets and courts I must say looked squalid." (Shaw, 2011)

A mud hut in Cross Walks

Lye Waste itself was described as a *"brow covered with clay-built cottages, both single and in irregular groups, rising above the straggling street"* (Anonymous)

Their houses lacked planned, sanitation and clean water (Linell, 2008)

Mud Hut, Cross Walks

The 1840s saw Lye Waste as a place of tumble down mud and brick houses (Neale, 2011) and was labeled the poorest area in the Stourbridge Poor Law union in 1872.

But Greenwood (1874) actually states that the roads were not unclean and each house had a smithy by the side. Again perhaps showing that the people of Lye Waste were misunderstood and living in horrible squalor but still working hard, rather than the immoral, lawless people they were often described as.

In 1884, mud huts were still in evidence in Lye Waste. And the last mud houses were only demolished in the 1960s. (Lane 2008)

Skeldings Lane, Lye

Crime in Lye Waste

Bad things did happen in Lye Waste – to say the least. Family fights and feuds were common (Neale, 2011), with some dragging on for years. There were some decent people in Lye Waste, but others would commit violence easily.

In 1796, Thomas Hill became the High Sheriff of Worcestershire. That year, there were more than 220 capitol crimes, including horse and sheep stealing, burning ricks, assault, coining and highway robbery. The punishments were severe, including execution. It is interesting to note that executions were carried out on Gallow's Days, which was later shortened to Gala Days.

Uriah Baker

Uriah Baker was born in 1835 on the Waste, near the Springfield Avenue and Perrins Lane of today. He was good with his fist and had a bad reputation. His first wife was Mary Wheale. She died between 1861 and 1863, amidst rumours of brutality, but Baker was not charged with anything. He had a long standing feud with the Hill family. Ann, the Hill's mother died in 1864 and some of her children returned for the funeral. A few days later an argument broke out in the beerhouse with locals, including Uriah Baker. There was a massive punch up. Thomas Hill was thrown down an embankment, another was hit by a missile on the head – a brick! Baker was listed as the brick thrower and Benjamin Hill, the victim, died a few days later. Baker was charged with Manslaughter and sent to Worcester. There were no witnesses, so the only thing that could be proved was wounding. Baker was sentenced to six months (Neale, 2011).

In 1865, he remarried to a Mary Guest/Lloyd. Two years later he was found guilty of "wounding with intent to do grievous bodily harm". He was sentenced to seven years imprisonment, obviously for a very serious crime. He was released in 1873 and went to live in Halesowen rather than Lye, then on to Kidderminster as an agricultural labourer. (Neale, 2011)

Crime in the Mine Shafts

In 1830, it was reported that Michael Toll threw his pregnant wife down one of the shafts (Neale, 2011).

And a few months later, on 16th May, 1830, a similar crime occurred. Charles Wall was a Lye nailer. He threw a child Sarah/Sally Chance down a 240 foot shaft. Sarah/Sally was only four years old. Wall was seen walking the girl towards the shaft but not back again. Wall was due to marry the child's mother soon. She wasn't arrested as she hadn't been seen with Sarah/Sally. No one knows why he killed her (Neale, 2011).

Wall was said to show little emotion when condemned to death, until the judge ordered that he should be handed over to doctors for dissection, the all the colour drained from his face (Neale, 2011).

John Phipson and the White Hod Rod

Another case is that of John Phipson. He was a nailer. There was a disagreement over drinking water from Elizabeth Millward's jug. She threw waste material from nail making at Phipson. He threw some back and the situation escalated until he threw a white hot rod from the furnace at Elizabeth. The metal penetrated her ribs and severed her aorta. She died shortly after. Phipson argued he did not remember throwing the iron. He was sent to trial in 1856 at Worcester Assizes. Phipson claimed it was accidental! The judge found him guilty and sentenced him to two weeks in solitary confinement.

Battling Beauties

Violence could break out in Lye Waste if people did not see eye to eye. The following was reported in the Brierley Hill Advertiser in 1857 (Black Country Bugle User, 2004)

"Sarah Garbett and Sarah Thorp, Lye Waste beauties, were charged with assaulting and beating a young woman named Matilda Round who was a newcomer to the place. It appeared that some jealousy had sprung up between the two parties and this passion finally flared up in a pitched battle out in the street. Round was knocked down, beaten severely, and kicked repeatedly on different parts of the body. She however, managed, with the assistance of a neighbour who was attracted by her cries, to escape with a couple of black eyes. In court the defendants had denied ever seeing Round on the night in question. Mrs Garbett, in answer to the charge, could only say that she was the mother of eleven children, a fact she took care to impress on the bench no fewer than eleven times. The Bench said, even though she was the mother of eleven children, she was showing her family a bad example, and they believed them to be a bad lot altogether.

The bench found them guilty as charged, fining Mrs. Garbett 5s. and Thorp half-a-crown, or in default twenty-one days hard labour. On hearing this the two women became very turbulent, and swore they would not pay a farthing. They were removed from the dock swearing at both witnesses and complainant".

Infanticide

Perhaps this is not the worst crime of all in Lye Waste. We have already heard that the people of Lye Waste were lawless, but just how lawless? There are stories of the people of Lye Waste feeding their unwanted babies to pigs or paying baby farmers to take their babies of their hands (Shaw, 2013). Infanticide was common in the 18th and 19th centuries in deprived areas in Britain. Families were often so poor, they could not cope with another mouth to feed.

"*The Lye Waste was a savage district, busy with chainmaking for pits [...] This Lye Waste boasted that coroners' inquests on infanticide were unknown in its area. There was some truth in the vaunt, despite the notorious immorality of the district; but the solution was simple. Most Lye Wasters kept pigs; if there chanced to be a superfluous baby, the family pig was kept on short commons for a day or so. Then the infant (somehow) fell into the sty! If a squealing was heard for an instant, phonetically it was interpreted as porcine ejaculation, and in half an hour no coroner could have found any remains to 'sit' upon.*""

(Woodgate, 1856 quoted in Shaw, 2010)

Whilst infant mortality was high at the time, it was particularly high in Lye.

> "*It was said that the situation was so bad that babies were actually fed to the Lye Wasters' pigs, thus avoiding any inquest.*" (Workman, 2010).

So we cannot really tell if live babies were fed to the pigs, or babies who had already died were.

Baby Farming

Baby Farming was also a common practice. Babies were "adopted" for a lump sum. These children were then often neglected and allowed to die, or even killed by their foster parents. Amelia Dyer was an infamous baby farmer who was thought to have murdered over 400 babies. She hung for her crimes in 1896 (Shaw, 2010).

Whilst we cannot know if these stories are true, it does show that the people of Lye Waste were considered to be so immoral they would be considered capable of such a terrible crime.

Industry

The people of Lye Waste were hard working. The civil war in England led to an increase in the need for iron products and the people of Lye Waste working hard to produce those goods. Within one hundred years of them settling in Lye Waste, it was an area of high trade and industry. Greenwood also commented that there was a smithy attached to every house.

The 1781, Enclosures Act allowed nailers' cottages to become freehold on seized land.

"In the early 18th century the last of the open fields had been enclosed by private agreements, but the commons had to await private Enclosure Acts that were enacted in 1780 and 1782. The four main commons were divided into enclosed plots of land and they consisted of Stourbridge Common (including The Heath), The Short Heath, High Park, and Lye Waste, amounting to some 700 acres in total. These commons all previously belonged to the Foley family as lords of the manor. The freehold was either sold to the tenants, exchanged for other pieces of land, or granted as compensation to those persons who had lost their grazing rights." (Perry, quoted in Turton, 2008).

A large part of the industry of Lye Waste was nailing, but besides making nails, glass was also produced and later, fire bricks and iron products were made in the area (Neale, 2011). Stourbridge is well known for the glass trade and a Hungarian Glassmaker, Henzvil Henzey found that the clay was very like that in Hungary. He set up small glasses houses in what is now known as Hungary Hill.

But the life of a nailer was a hard one. A popular song at the time had the first line of –

"From morn till night, from early light, we toil for little pay … "(Workman, 2010).

The nailers worked for very little, but still they were exploited. They worked in cramped hot conditions, often two or three families living and working in small workshops, sometimes just 10 feet square. Many could hardly afford to buy food (Workman 2010).

A report from the "Illustrated Midlands News" quoted by Workman (2010) states that a family of nailers

"did not know the taste of meat; they mostly had a cup of tea and some bread for breakfast and dinner, little else …"

The life of the nailers and their children was harsh, but still they were exploited by foggers or middlemen or the tommy shop or truck system. Basically the nailers were forced to buy their iron on credit from foggers. The foggers then bought the nails back from them with tokens or cheques that could only be spent in the fogger's shop or pub! It is easy to imagine why the nailers went on strike several times (Workman, 2010).

Another song from the time quoted in Workman (2010)

> *"Oh, the slaves abroad in the sugar cane,*
>
> *Find plenty of help to pity their pain,*
>
> *But the slaves at home in the mine or fire,*
>
> *Have plenty to pity but none to admire".*

By 1832, the fire clay of Lye Waste was in great demand and by the 1840s, women were hand moulding fire bricks at a rate of around a 1000 per day and earning the grand total of 4 shillings (about 20 pence).

You can imagine the industry of the area and the noise –

"Tink, tink, tink, louder still, and now you come within sight of Lye Waste Village and its thousand fires, and its cruelly hard-worked and badly paid colony of nail-makers"

(Greenwood, 1874).

But the import of cheap nails from Belguim started in 1837 and led to unrest in the Lye nailers, leading to the Nailers' Riots of 1842.

This was a time when an already poor group of people became even poorer.

The nailers carried out strikes many times over the next few years. The 1840s became known as the "Hungry 40s" (Cochrane, 2013).

In the late 1850s the nail strike continued and the Wood Brothers arrange for a sheep roasting to help 36 old people and poor widows (Pritchard).

During the Nailers' Strike of 1862, a man called Joseph Pearson would not strike. Other strikers threatened to "stop his wind". Days later, a group of men invaded his nail shop and cut Pearson's bellows to ribbons.

This meant he could not blow his furnace to heat iron roads, so he was forced to join the strikers (Neale, 2011).

The winter of 1869 was distressing for the nailers, 500 loaves were handed out a week, but many remained unfed. But if you consider that in 1877, the population of Lye Waste was thought to be 5786, 500 loaves a week is not a lot. Also consider that in 1872, Lye had already been labeled as one of the poorest areas in the Stourbridge Poor Law Union and we can see the poverty and hardship the nailers and their families would have experienced.

On the 11th January, 1879, Reverends Fletcher, Wright and Broderick distributed 80 gallons of soup and 350 loaves of bread. On the 25th January, this rose to 1500 loaves and 400 gallons of soup.

By the 1840s, the handmade nail industry was declining, leading to hardship for the nailers, but other industry began to replace it, such as chain making and bucket making, leading to Lye Being known as the Bucket Capital of the World (Dunn, 1999).

The workers of the area continued to produce fire bricks. By 1852, 14 million bricks were produced, using 46000 tons of clay. By 1864, it was 30 million bricks and by 1874, 258, 792 tons of fire clay had been extracted. Before 1860, 75% of the brickworks work force were women and 50% were under 10.

Children And Work

Nailing took around seven years to learn apparently, but in reality this was often because young children were used to work in the trade, often as young as eight. Most were waifs and strays from the local Poor House. The children were taken on as apprentices and often worked with the nail maker until they were 21 or in some cases 24.

Children had often been seen as cheap labour by the nail masters. It was common to see young children working to bring more money into their home. But this "often had serious implications, and there were frequent accidents involving young children. This went hand in hand with high infant mortality, with a medical officer reporting a high death rate among children under five. He put it down to *"the habit of the mothers leaving their children unattended while they were engaged in the nail shop"*. A situation the unfortunate mothers were, generally, powerless to avoid. (Workman, 2010)

"As most couldn't read, they would have had little understanding of the slavery they were about to undergo. So who were the men who took advantage of this system, and trawled the poor houses of the region looking for likely candidates." (Neale, 2011).

It was not only the nailers who used children in this way, glass manufacturers and local farmers also did.

Before 1860, 75% of the brickworks work force were women and 50% were under 10.

The following article by Greenwood (1874) gives a good picture of the life of the people and children of Lye Waste.

"The pedestrian explorer of odd places in and about Staffordshire would, in the event of his approaching either Netherton, Rowley, Lye Waste, or Bromsgrove on a Saturday afternoon, encounter a spectacle that might rather puzzle him: a straggling procession of men and women and children, the majority of the former sober, but a few of them drunk, and one and all so scantily and shabbily dressed that their poverty-stricken state of existence is at once made known. Each of them is carrying a number of iron wands like a bundle of withies for weaving, but secured in the grip of a twist of iron wire, instead of by a green osier twig — rods of various lengths, from four feet to ten, and of different sizes, from that of a man's little finger to the thin end of a tobacco-pipe.

The lighter loads are in the custody of children, chiefly boys, but some of them girls, and varying in age from seven upwards, each one shouldering its property, and trudging along at a sedate pace, with a countenance expressive of the practice of mental arithmetic under difficulties, the key to which was to be found in iron rods past and iron rods present; little old men and women, looking rather like adults growing down than children growing up; grizzled old handicraftsmen and women in pinafores; children used to fire and forge, hairsinged and smutty, and with their dimples showing like wrinkles with the grime of smithy smoke that traced them; youngsters whose boots showed their upper leathers singed and scarred with falling chips of red-hot metal, and with hands that, according to nature, should not have advanced beyond the round and chubby stage, corned and bumped at the knuckles, and with the nails worn down like those of a file-grinder.

"The puzzled explorer would naturally be curious to ascertain of what kind of mothers such children could be born. There they are — the women who come toiling down the road, sometimes with a load of rods on one arm, and on the other a baby drawing nourishment from a breast so smutty and rusty looking as to give rise to the idea that it must be gritty with iron filings.

"Women well able to carry such a double load, however. The size of their arms is prodigious. Here comes along one laden with baby and iron, a wizen-faced woman, lank as a plank and about as symmetrical, but whose bared right arm and the fist terminating it might belong to a prizefighter — a brown fist with a broad thumb, and an arm with sinews standing out like tanned cord; and a muscle for the woman, like the majority, wears her gown-sleeve 'tucked up' as a male mechanic wears his shirtsleeve that bulges to the size of a penny-roll.

"Let the puzzled explorer bottle up his curiosity, and come this way again say, to Lye Waste, on Monday, for an explanation. Let his visit be deferred until dusk of evening or later, and this is the picture that Lye Waste will show him.

"First, though, as to sound. Lye Waste is a village of considerable dimensions, stowed away and hidden from the main road; but before it is reached, dark though it may be, you are made aware that it is not far off. The very air seems to tingle with a tinkling, not a loud banging and ringing of lusty full-grown hammers and anvils, but a kind of infantine clamour of the sort, as though this was the nursery of hammers and anvils, and rare play was going on amongst the youngsters.

Tink, tink, tink, thousands of hammers, thousands of anvils, and no more real noise than six Woolwich farriers might any day in the week be backed to make if they would but give their shoulders to it. Tink, tink, tink, louder still, and now you come within sight of Lye Waste Village and its thousand fires, and its cruelly hard-worked and badly paid colony of nail-makers.

"One of the quaintest sights that can be conceived, and well worth the contemplation of those who delight in discussing the 'rights of women' and whose tender sensibilities are shocked that the gentle sex should engage in such masculine employments as setting up printing types or fixing together the tiny wheels of a watch.

These are the tender-hearted souls who are scandalized by the knowledge that in France and other barbarous countries women frequently perform the drudgery here assigned to the commonest of labourers street sweeping, brick and mortar carrying, etc. Did they never hear of the female blacksmiths of Staffordshire? There are not a hundredth part of them here at Lye Waste, which may boast of a thousand at least.

You may count them any night, for there is no shyness or delicacy in the matter. Here in the village are rows and whole streets of smithy hovels, and the fronts are wide open, and there you may observe them. If you like to 'stand' a can of beer, you may enter the smithy and have a chat with them — but idle only on your part.

Time is too precious when a woman, stripped like a man from wrist to shoulder, must face the forge for fourteen hours a day before a shilling may be earned.

"I cannot help repeating that, coming on it for the first time, it is one of the strangest sights in the world. The streets of Lye Waste are narrow and not unclean; and, as before stated, by the side of every house is a smithy, and each one contains from two to five 'stalls' or 'hearths,' as each fire is called; and at night-time the light is so great that streetlamps are rendered a superfluity. By the ruddy glow that streams out from the numerous hearths, it would be quite easy to find a pin dropped in the middle of the street.

"Whole families work in these smithies. It is nothing uncommon to find a mother and her three lusty daughters, fully of marriageable age, stripped to their stays, and, with a kerchief over their shoulders, wielding the hammers and tugging at the bellows, and working away with a will, amongst the banging and roaring and spark-flying, and singing as merrily as larks, if not as melodiously.

Children, too — the youngsters that the puzzled explorer met last Saturday. The rods they and their parents carried were nail-rods; and here they are, the small Vulcans, sweating over an anvil, set up according to their stature, making brads. Pale little wretches, most of them, the firelight betraying with cruel fidelity their haggard, unchildish faces, each one wistful and anxious with the consciousness that bread to eat must first be earned. It appeared odd enough to see the women standing in the smithy ashes with a big hammer in their fist; but it was infinitely more painful to watch these tiny brad makers, with a wisp of rag round their heads to keep the baby growth of hair out of their eyes, straightening their small backs and spitting on their palms before they grasped the hammer to make the most of the last 'heat.' "The hearths or stalls are not the property of the nailmakers; they are rented at the rate fourpence a week each, the landlord finding the fireplace and bellows.

I saw some 'treadle hammers,' connected with anvils, that struck me as being very ingenious, although the working of them must be cruelly hard work for a woman.

"As with other blacksmithing, there must be two hammers used on a piece of red-hot iron, a small one to polish and a big one to beat. In the instances I allude to, the big hammer was hung at a convenient height above the anvil, and connected with a treadle such as is attached to a knife-grinder's wheel on the ground. I saw an old woman making nails in this single-handed fashion in a manner that would have been diverting were it not for the knowledge of how severely her old limbs must be taxed. She would bring a 'heat' from the fire, clap it on the anvil, and with her left hand manoeuvring the nail about, her right hand striking it with the small hammer, she thrust out a foot and vigorously worked the treadle; and as the big hammer worked up and down, clump-clump, her aged head kept time with it, till it seemed that the whole machinery was convulsed with the throes of dissolution, and must presently fly all to pieces."

(Greenwood, 1874)

These children were working hard in horrible conditions to earn a pittance.

Changes in public opinion during Victorian times regarding work carried out by children eventually led to the number of cheap labour available drying up for the nailers. In 1870, the Factories Act, meant that 10,000 children who were employed in the brickyards were sent home or to school. (Workman, 2010), although children were still working in harsh conditions decades later.

Women

We have mentioned children and women previously, but just to focus on the women briefly. Theirs was obviously a hard life, caring for their children in difficult conditions, the high mortality rates and having to work. We have already mentioned that in the 1840s, women were hand moulding fire bricks at a rate of 1000 per day for 4 shillings (about 20 pence). And before 1860, 75% of the brickworks work force were women and 50% were under 10.

A story that brings it into perspective – In 1872, a factory inspector saw a girl carrying clay. She looked ill and he thought she had been drinking the night before. He said to her –

" Yoe doe look up to much this morning." She replied, "Neither would yoe if yo had had a babi in the night."

And whilst working, they still had to watch their children. Cochrane (2013) states that

> *"Most were uneducated, ill-mannered, and described as a lawless society, often seen semi-naked as they scratched a meagre living in their workshops, making nails from dawn till dusk.*

Men, women and children from an early age, and even babbies (babies) were reared in the nail shops under the watchful eye of the mother as she worked at the anvil."

Church

If Lye Waste was such a lawless area, we wonder if a church was to be found. Indeed Neale (2011) says

"….it was a brave Clergyman who first set foot on the Waste. Indeed, the Unitarian Chapel was not built until 1790, and faced fierce competition from the many Beer Houses that had sprang up".

Many church missionaries came to Lye Waste hoping to improve the people there. They were often met with short shrift and occasionally violent assault before being driven off (Shaw, 2010).

But in 1791, services were well attended in Lye Waste, according to Cochrane, 2013. This was the same year as attacks on Presbyterian Dissenters in Birmingham and Lye. So plans to build a chapel were put on hold in Lye Waste, but a building was leased for 7 years for worship. In 1806, the Presbyterian Chapel was opened.

In 1809, George Wood was encouraging people to worship in Lye Cross House, but this moved unsuccessfully to a larger warehouse, which probably lead to the first Unitarian Church on the Waste. The First Unitarian/Presbyterian Chapel was established in Lye Waste. The minister was Reverend James Scott. The chapel cost £245, 14s 9d. Interesting in that, until 1813, it was actually a penal offence to be Unitarian. The people of Lye Waste obviously did things *their* way.

In 1818, John Wesley, a non-conformist minister, held a meeting to bring locals out of their *"spiritual darkness"* (Cochrane, 2013). Hecklers and a mob with sticks attended another meeting and dragged the preacher out.

A Wesleyan chapel was built in Lye Waste in 1822.

In 1829, Reverend James Scott died. He became known as the Apostle of Lye Waste. But by the 1851 Census, it was reported that there were 130 men and 10 women over 80. It also record that the total population was 5901 and of that figure 44% were church goers. Of that 44%, 70% were Methodists.

In 1870, a festival was organized in Hagley Park to raise funds for a Temperance Hall in Lye. Three to four thousand people attended, and it raised £20.

Education

In 1782, Waste Bank School was founded from a £3200 endowment from Thomas Hill.

In 1813, Thomas Hill thought the people of Lye Waste needed to be civilised so he bought a church and a school, building it from clay bricks, using clay from the site the school was built on. (Cochrane, 2013) The first School was built on the site of Belmont Mission by Thomas Hill and was built using bricks from Fimbrell Glass House. It was called Mrs Batchelor's School as she was married to the owner of Fimbrell's Glass House. (Cochrane, 2013)

When Lye School was first opened, there was a lack of road names according to Perrins and "it was obviously that strangers would have trouble locating the residents". Perrins argues that many of the streets names were from local residents. Cochrane (2013) also points out that they tended to use nicknames rather than their actual names. Nicknames included "Tay Pots" (tea pots to the non-Lye speaker), "Bug Connop" and "Split Pays" (split peas). Cochrane believes that this is how Connop's Lane in Lye got its name.

Connops Lane, Lye

Leisure

You might wonder if the people of Lye Waste had any time for leisure, but bull baiting was apparently common in the area and in 1866, there were 7000 people living in Lye and Lye Waste, served by 53 pubs.

*"For many generations, the inhabitants of **Lye Waste,** went about the busy task of earning enough to pay for the beer. Well, that's not really fair I suppose, there were those amongst them who had higher standards, and actually bought food as well. You can't after all, swing a hammer, dig coal, or make bricks, when half starved can you?"* (Neale, 2011)

Jasper (2010) argues that perhaps Lye had the most pubs in the British Isles and quotes a visitor in to Lye at the time –

" *Whilst on a visit to the Lye District, it surprised me to see the "Brickmakers Arms" carrying the "Swan With Two Necks" headed by The Crown" and place him under the "Royal Oak." Proud I might be in witnessing the "Spread Eagle" fly over the "Windmill" and roost on the sign of "The Mitre" later on.*

I was surprised to see him carry the "Old Cross" from the front of the "New Rose and Crown" and walk off "Seven Stars" on the "Malt Shovel" by the light of the "Rising Sun" and defied "The Bull's Head" while he was searching for "The Fox" which had taken shelter in "The Noah's Ark."

Little did I think "The Dove" would "Anchor" him down at "The Vine" while "The White Horse" was bringing up "The Queens Head" as quiet as "The Lamb" and get permission from "The George" to place the "Three Crowns" on the head of "The Duke of York" whilst he was holding a "Bunch of Grapes," but the most interesting feature was to see him come through the "Holly Bush" without a scratch, and missing "The Vine," run down to "The Railway" carrying "The Beefeaters" who were wearing "The Unicorn" in defiance of the "Crown."

Just then the "Bell" rang for "The Hare and Hounds" to be chased by "The Red Lion" over the "Cross Walks" by the light of "The Star" past "The Hundred House" to capture him at "The Talbot."

After I had a drink at "The Balds Lane Tavern" I arranged for a man to carry the "Anvil" to "The Castle." He had a rest at "The Pear Tree" and crossing over to the "Saltbrook End" he saw a fight between "The Peacock" and "The Swan" who had been matched by the "Oddfellows" under the "Royal Oak."

Watching him was "Lord Dudley Arms," who had a "Falcon" and was standing by "The Vine" and, after finding a "New Inn," ordered the "Old Bell" to be tolled as "The Coach and Horses" came down by "The Queensway" to have a "Union" at the "Foxcote" and so ended my visit to Lye."

Fifty three pubs for 7000 people sounds an awful lot, but given their hard lives, we have to forgive them for the occasional tipple I think.

Conclusion

In 1800, Birmingham Ministers said *"there is no more rude or uncultivated spot in the whole of the British Isles"* (Dunn, 1999).

But gradually Lye Waste changed. The mud huts were replaced with long rows of terraced cottages, some even remain today, despite the redevelopment of Lye.

Elihu Burritt (1860 quoted in Jaspar, 2010) reported in 1860 how Lye Waste had changed.

> *"I came upon a broad, smoky valley and there stands the populous district of Lye Waste, which a few years ago was part of heathendom, with a population brutally vicious and ignorant; but is now, by means of schools and itinerant preachers, showing signs of morality and civilisation..."*

Lye Waste flourished with the township developing further. Large families were the norm. Healthy couples often had 12 or more children (Jasper 2010).

Churches were built and shops appeared. And of course, the pubs!

Lye Waste Book References

Anonymous – This information was taken from a photocopied chapter of a book. The chapter title is the Hamlets of Oldswinford. I have not been able to find the author or the actual book that this photocopy is from.

Black Country Bugle User (2004) Turbulent Times in Lye. **www.blackcountrybugle.co.uk/turbulent-times-in-lye-waste/story-201204413-detail/story.html**

Black Country Bugle User A (2004) The Rowley Regis Nailer and ringleader of the Dudley Riots of 1842 **http://www.blackcountrybugle.co.uk/Rowley-Regis-nailer-ringleader-Dudley-Riots-1842/story-20121059-detail/story.html**

Black Country Bugle User (2009) Paupers regaled with roast beef and plum pudding **http://www.blackcountrybugle.co.uk/Paupers-regaled-roast-beef-plum-pudding/story-20133651-detail/story.html**

Cochrane, D. (2013) A Brief History of Lye and Wollescote, Part II. M.J.Cochrane, Publishers.

Cochrane, D. (2007) The History of the Hill Family of Oldnall, Dennis, Lye and others. M.J. Cochrane, Publishers.

Dunn P. (1999) Lye and Wollescote. A Second Selection. Sutton Publishing Ltd

Dunn P. and Wooldridge C. (2013) Lye and Wollescote – A Fourth Selection. The History Press.

Greenwood J. (1874) In The Black Country. From The Dictionary of Victorian London. Viewed at **http://www.victorianlondon.org/publications4/strange-28.htm** (accessed 18.7.14)

Halesowen Roots (2008) Lye Waste. **http://www.rootschat.com/forum/index.php?topic=250828.msg2256138#msg2256138**

Hutton (1806) as cited in Jasper J. (2013) Some History and Ales Houses of Old Lye. **http://www.blackcountrybugle.co.uk/History-Ale-Houses-old-Lye/story-20155591-detail/story.html**

Jasper J. (2013) Some History and Ales Houses of Old Lye. **http://www.blackcountrybugle.co.uk/History-Ale-Houses-old-Lye/story-20155591-detail/story.html**

Lane J. (2004) Forum Chat **http://archiver.rootsweb.ancestry.com/th/read/ENG-BLACK-COUNTRY/2004-09/1096538421**

Linell (2008) Lye Waste.

http://www.rootschat.com/forum/index.php?topic=250828.msg2256138#msg2256138

Neale D. (2011) – Quote from forum chat –

http://www.blackcountrymuse.com/apps/forums/topics/show/4860630

MBSGH – Lye http://www.worcesterbmsgh.co.uk/parish/lye (accessed 18.7.14)

Perrins W. (unknown) Humour, Dialect, Nicknames, Social Habits, Customs, Songs and Poems. Publishers Unknown.

Wooldridge G. Quoted in Perrins (Unknown) – The Beauties of Lye Waste - (Copied from a selection of poetry by Cradley Bag Pudding, 1873 printed by J. T. Ford, Stourbridge, 1873, reproduced in Perrins).

Pritchard E. (unknown) The Making of Lye (1850 – 1900). Self published.

Shaw D. (2011) "Small Vulcans – Sweating over an anvil" The Child Nailmakers of Lye Waste.

http://www.blackcountrybugle.co.uk/Small-Vulcans-sweating-anvil-child-nailmakers-Lye-Waste/story-20146396-detail/story.html

Shaw D. (2013)   Trip back in time to Lye in the 1900s
http://www.blackcountrybugle.co.uk/Trip-time-Lye-
1900s/story-20257561-detail/story.html

Vestigan – quoted in Hamlets of Oldswinford – This is a
photocopied article. The actual book title and author are
unknown, despite research.

Weston J. and Price M. (2010) The Lye and Wollescote
Cemetery and Chapels – A Victorian Cemetery and its Notable
Burials. West Midlands Historical Buildings Trust.

Woodgate (1856) quoted in Shaw D. (2011) "Small Vulcans –
Sweating over an anvil" The Child Nailmakers of Lye Waste.
http://www.blackcountrybugle.co.uk/Small-Vulcans-
sweating-anvil-child-nailmakers-Lye-Waste/story-
20146396-detail/story.html

Wooldridge G. Quoted in Perrins (Unknown) – The Beauties
of Lye Waste - (Copied from a selection of poetry by Cradley
Bag Pudding, 1873 printed by J. T. Ford, Stourbridge, 1873,
reproduced in Perrins).

Wootton, M. (2008) Forum comment.
http://www.rootschat.com/forum/index.php?topic-250828.m
sg2271057#msg2271057 (10.12.08)

Workman J (2010) Children "at Werk" in the Black Country. Black Country Bugle.

http://www.blackcountrybugle.co.uk/Childrenat-Werk-Black-Country/story-20144131-detail/story.html

CPSIA information can be obtained
at www.ICGtesting.com
Printed in the USA
LVOW02s0152060416
482266LV00020B/551/P